MADE IN THE
U.S.A.

TEDDY BEARS

From Start to Finish

TANYA LEE STONE

PHOTOGRAPHS BY GALE ZUCKER

BLACKBIRCH PRESS, INC.
WOODBRIDGE, CONNECTICUT

For my mom, who gave me Brownie, my first
teddy bear. —TLS

Special Thanks
The author and publisher would like to thank Cal Workman,
Kathleen Straube, Larry Rushford, Kathy French, and Beth Ann
Pickett for their generous help in putting this project together.

Published by Blackbirch Press, Inc.
260 Amity Road
Woodbridge, CT 06525

e-mail: staff@blackbirch.com
Web site: www.blackbirch.com

©2000 by Blackbirch Press, Inc.
First Edition

Printed in Singapore

10 9 8 7 6 5 4 3 2 1

Photo Credits: All photographs ©Gale Zucker except pages: 4: ©Alan
Jakubek; page 24 ©Natalie Stultz; page 29 (top right): ©Rose McNulty.

If you would like to see teddy bears made, come to The Vermont
Teddy Bear Factory in Shelburne, Vermont. For information,
call (800) 829-BEAR or log onto the company web site
www.VermontTeddyBear.com.

Library of Congress Cataloging-in-Publication Data
Stone, Tanya Lee.
Teddy bears: from start to finish /by Tanya Lee Stone: photographs by Gale
Zucker
    p.   cm. — (Made in the U.S.A.)
    Includes bibliographical references and index.
    Summary: Photographs and text describe step-by-step process by which
teddy bears are made at the Vermont Teddy Bear Company.
    ISBN 1-56711-479-2
    1. Soft toy making. 2. Teddy bears. [1. Teddy bears. 2. Soft toy mak-
ing.] I. Zucker, Gale, ill. II. Title. III. Series.
TT174.3   .S76 2000
688.7'243—dc21   00-008393

CONTENTS

Is there a teddy bear in your house? People have cuddled them since 1902. That was the year President Theodore Roosevelt went hunting for a bear.

As the story goes, a bear cub was tied to a tree for the president. Instead of shooting the bear, Teddy Roosevelt saved its life. A shopkeeper's wife then made a bear and called it "Teddy's Bear." The shopkeeper hung it in his shop window. It was the first American teddy bear.

Since then, teddy bears have become some of the world's most popular items for kids to cuddle— and adults, too! On the pages that follow, you'll see how these cute and cuddly creatures are created, from beginning to end.

 Teddy bears come in every shape, size, and color.

BUNCHES OF BEARS

The Vermont Teddy Bear Company® is the biggest maker of hand-crafted bears in North America. They make more than 100 different kinds of bears and bear outfits. Each year, hundreds of thousands of teddy bears are made. If you stood them on top of each other, the bears could probably reach the moon!

The Vermont Teddy Bear Company is located in Shelburne, Vermont.

The Bear Facts

John Sortino started the Vermont Teddy Bear Company in 1981 after making a bear for his son Graham. He sold the bears from a cart on Church Street in Burlington, Vermont.

A karate bear is almost ready for its new home.

🐾

Head designer Kathleen Straube works on colors and fabrics for a new bear.

THE DRAWING BOARD

How does the The Vermont Teddy Bear Company® create so many kinds of bears? Each bear starts as an idea from a brainstorming session in the design department. People from other parts of the company also share their ideas. They talk about different types of fur and clothing. They also make lists of possible names for the bears.

The designers draw sketches and create patterns for making bear outfits. They also choose just the right fabric and trim. Then a seamstress makes a prototype. A prototype is a sample, or model, of what a final bear will look like.

The designers experiment with many fabrics, trims, and furs.

A FURRY BEGINNING

Once a new bear design is approved, it goes into production. The first step is laying out the fabric for the bear's body. The material that is used as fur is rolled onto a table and cut to fit. It takes two people to pull the fabric and inspect it. The first layer is placed furry side down. The next layer is placed furry side up. This way, each bear will have a left side and a right side. Twelve to fourteen layers of fabric are pulled onto the table and all cut at once.

A large roll of furry material is ready to be pulled onto the table.

Left: *This table holds enough material to make 210 teddy bears.*
Above: *Workers lay out fabric, cut it to the right length, and inspect it.*

Dies are placed, then the press comes down and punches them through the material.

A CUT ABOVE

Next, the layered fur is pulled onto the cutting surface and lined up. Then metal molds, called dies, are placed on the fabric. Dies are like cookie cutters. Each die is shaped like a bear part. A press is used to punch the dies through all the layers. (The pressure from the press is equal to about 12 elephants sitting on the dies!) The pieces are sorted before they go to the sewing department.

Above: *Leg pieces are banded together.*
Right: *A worker holds up a layer of fabric with different pieces cut out.*
Below: *A metal die and the cut pieces that will make a brown bear.*

IN STITCHES

To make about 600 bears a day, the sewing department needs 18 workers. Each day, a stitcher works on two or three parts. Some do bodies and arms, some sew heads, and others work on foot pads and leg seams.

The sewing department works together as a team.

Above: *A stitcher sews a leg together.*
Right: *Another stitcher works on part of a head.*

HEADS UP!

There are many steps to sewing a teddy head. First, the top part of the nose is sewn into a head piece, also called a gusset. Then, in a step called set and tack, two sides of a head are held and the ears are sewn in. The two head sides are then sewn into the gusset and the eyes are put in. Next, the sides of the nose are sewn into the chin seam. This is called chinning. Finally, the head is turned right-side out.

A pile of inside-out heads are waiting to be "chinned."

Above: *Teddy bear eyes are punched in place.*
Right: *A completed teddy bear head is "turned" right-side out on a pole.*

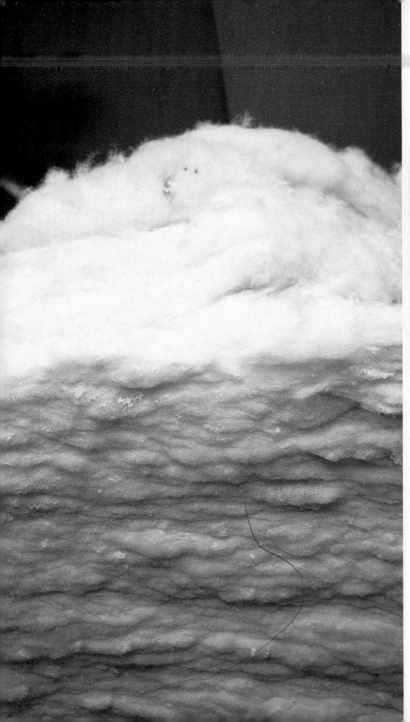

Left: *Stuffing is tightly packed before it enters the picker.*
Below: *A worker loads stuffing into a picker.*

ALL STUFFED UP

The sewn teddy bear parts are now ready to be stuffed. Stuffing material is fed into a picker that separates fibers. Then a large machine called a hopper is filled with stuffing and pumped into stuffing machines. Heads, legs, and arms get stuffed before going to the assembly department to be put together.

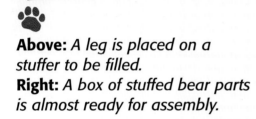

Above: *A leg is placed on a stuffer to be filled.*
Right: *A box of stuffed bear parts is almost ready for assembly.*

Bears Make Fun Messengers

The Vermont Teddy Bear Company is famous for their Bear-Gram® gift delivery service. From anywhere in the world, people can visit their web site or call the shop to pick out and dress a gift bear. If someone wants to welcome a new baby, he or she can have a bear sent wearing a diaper and bib with the baby's name on it. For someone's birthday, a bear could wear a party hat and blow a horn. For Halloween, a bear can be dressed up in a skeleton costume holding a pumpkin filled with treats. Or, if a favorite friend loves to ski, a bear can be dressed in a snowsuit and hat with a pair of skis. A name can even be embroidered on many outfits to make the bear more personal. There are so many choices, it can be hard to decide on one! Luckily, Bear Counselors at the company are always ready to help. It's a Vermont Teddy Bear tradition.

Above: *A worker uses skilled hands and a crochet hook to put a pin in a bear arm.*

A line of finished legs.

PINNING

The last step before final assembly is called pinning. Workers insert pins into the joints of the bears. The pins allow the arms and legs to move once the bear is finished.

19

PUTTING IT ALL TOGETHER

Once the joints are pinned, a bear is ready to be assembled. A special machine is used to press and secure each pin to a washer. First the legs are put on, then the arms, and finally, the teddy bear's head. Once a bear is all put together, it goes back to the stuffing room. There, the body is filled.

Above: *A worker is about to attach a bear's arm with the press.*
Right: *After the arms and legs are attached, the head is put on.*

Above: *This bear is all put together.*
Right: *The body of an assembled bear is stuffed.*

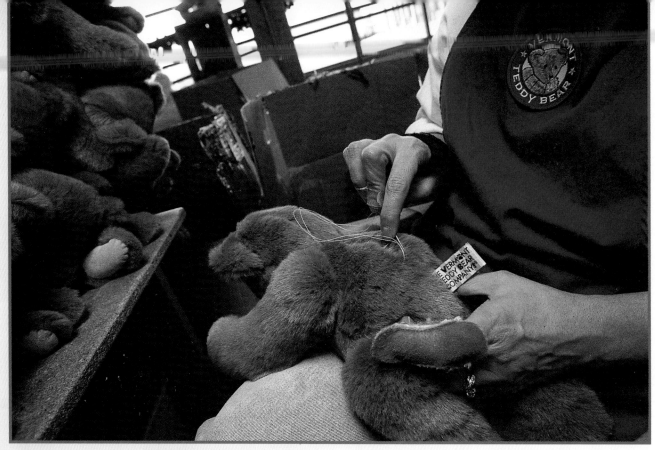

The back of a bear is sewn up.

THE FINISHING TOUCHES

At this stage of the process, the bears are all put together. But they're not finished yet! The assembled and stuffed bears now go to Bear Finishing. There, the backs are sewn up. Then the bears are inspected and brushed. Once this is done, the bears are ready to be dressed.

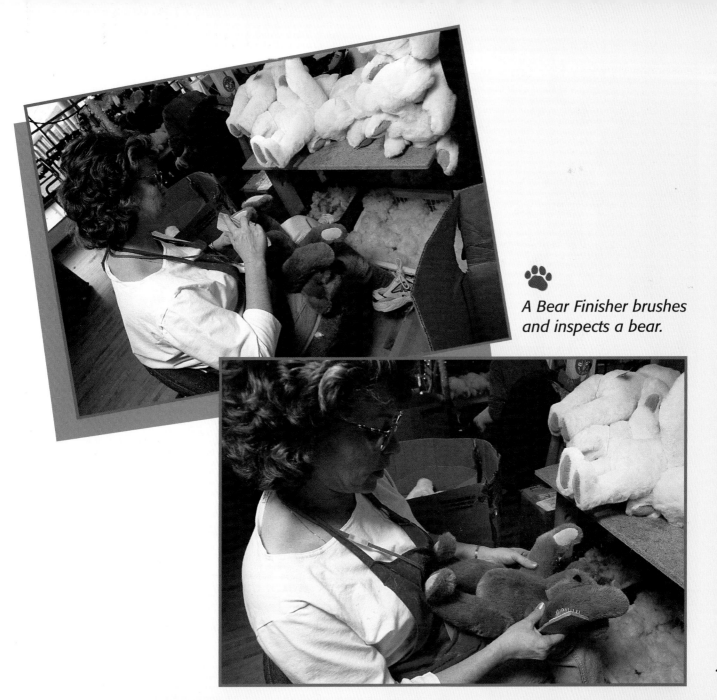

A Bear Finisher brushes and inspects a bear.

23

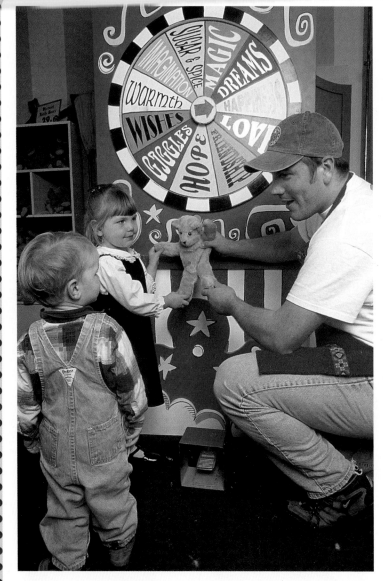

A Friend for Life

If you visit the Vermont Teddy Bear factory, you can make your very own bear. In the Make A Friend for Life® room, there are lots of choices to be made. First, you can select a bear with any kind of fur that you like. Then you spin the special stuffing wheel to add things like magic and dreams to your bear's stuffing.

Children get help from a Bear Ambassador while they choose their bear's special stuffing.

Make A Friend For Life!® Birth Certificate!

My new friend's name is: ....

Birth Date: ....

Birth Time: ....

I,........................ promise to live up to the Make A Friend For Life!® Code
and share all my adventures with my new friend.

*When **Make A Friend for Life**® bears are born, they are given birth certificates.*

Once your teddy is stuffed just the way you want it, you can help sew it up. Your bear is then given a birth certificate and the "Teddy Bear Oath" is said. Your bear is then brushed. After that, you get to pick out an outfit. It is even given a suitcase for traveling home!

BEAR WEAR

Making clothing is a big part of what happens at the factory. A computer is used to design the patterns. To make the clothes, a saw first cuts through thick layers of fabric. Stitchers in the clothing department make about 430 outfits a day. The completed outfits are then packed in kits.

Above left: *A pattern is used to cut fabric.*
Left: *Sewing an outfit.*
Below: *These items will be packed in kits for the Grandmother Bear.*

The embroidery machine at work.

Names and dates can also be embroidered on bear clothing. First, a special computer is programmed with the information. Then the item is placed into the embroidery machine.

PACKING FOR HOME

The final steps happen after someone orders a specific bear. Crates of bears and kits are stacked high. At the beginning of the fulfillment line, a computerized order shows which bear, clothing kit, and other items a customer has chosen. A worker "picks" everything out and layers orders in a bin. Once a bin is full, another worker clips each order to a box and fills it with the bear and its belongings.

Above: *A machine puts the boxes together.*
Right: *A variety of bear items.*

CSE000054
Soccer ball

CSE000048
Basketball

Above: *A bin full of embroidered bibs.*
Right: *A Worker gently places bears in boxes before they are dressed.*
Below: *Boxed bears head down the assembly line.*

A dresser gets a Birthday Bear ready to go.

BON VOYAGE

The boxes travel down the assembly line to workers called dressers. These workers take all the items out of a box and dress a bear in its outfit. Each bear is then packed back up, complete with a personal card and some candy. Once in its box, it will be shipped to its new home and its new owner, who eagerly awaits it somewhere in the world.

A Football Bear
gets dressed by a
teddy dresser.

GLOSSARY

Die a tool or device similar to a cookie cutter that cuts a shape or form from a material.

Gusset a piece of material used to expand or strengthen; in a teddy bear, the gusset is part of the head.

Hopper a container with a narrow opening at the bottom, used to hold material and empty it into another container.

Picker a machine used to pick apart fibers in tightly packed material.

Prototype an original model from which something is made.

Synthetic human-made material; not natural.

FOR MORE INFORMATION

Books

Erlbach, Arlene. *Teddy Bears* (Household History Series). Minneapolis, MN: Carolrhoda Books, 1997.

Mitgutsch, Ali. Marlene Reidel. Annegert Fuchshuber *From Idea to Toy* (Start to Finish Book). Minneapolis, MN: Carolrhoda Books, 1989.

Wulffson, Don. Laurie Keller. *Toys: Amazing Stories Behind Some Great Inventions.* New York, NY: Henry Holt & Company, Inc., 2000.

Web Site
The Vermont Teddy Bear Factory

Learn about the history of the company, take a mini-tour of the factory, and find out how to send a Bear-Gram—
www.vermontteddybear.com

INDEX